AF544841

LIMITED FIRST EDITION

Works by RICHARD TEVIS	*The Miracle at San Juan* *Juanita* *Chac - A Legendary History of the Maya* *Elfinhound*

ELFINHOUND

ELFINHOUND

RICHARD TEVIS

Illustrations by Shirley Holt

Manufactured in the United States of America.

First printing, 1984.

Published by Richard Tevis, Tres Amigos Publications, 26325 Carmelo, Carmel, California 93923.

Library of Congress Catalog Card Number 84-90217

ISBN 0-930277-01-5

For Sheila and John

ELFINHOUND

A gaunt owl watched.

Soon he would forage the woods in wind-whispered flight,

almost silent, talons readied for the strike.

Death would wait for darkness.

The boy was alone.

He had made his camp by a blackened tree. His cooking fire,

a meagre thing,

was a diamond in the ravaged waste of the forest.

The warm dusk was deepening.

The owl's eye reflected the fire as though a burning coal,

caught on a limb, hung suspended below the dark sky mass.

Seeing it, the boy was startled, then laughed.

He was the hunter watched by the hunter.
"Hello, friend," he called. "It's lonely here.
"Come join me."
The owl was motionless, waiting for the night's supremacy,
for the small creatures to show, if any remained.

The boy studied Orion,
conscious of the rancid smell of ash. He smoked the first,
letting his mind expand to the planet's course, to the
    galaxies,
to the ultimate finality.
Would it be the coming of ice, an airless void of desert,
or holocaust?
In the evolutionary chain, only man
has been given the power to destroy himself
    and all living things.
Only he can stop the planet's spin
    before its time.
The desolating blast of volcanic fury, sudden and absolute,

had dramatized the truth that man's existence is a transient
thing,
limited by the cosmic force that moves the universe.

The owl was hunting now,
searching the wasteland softened by a new moon's light,
night eyes alert to the kill.
The boy's thoughts came at random, vividly acute.
Why had the dead gods died, the living gods of the Maya?
The man-created gods whose pantheon was in the stars,
in the caverns of the dark and secret underworld.
Was man himself the slayer?
The boy's reverie was broken by a rush of air, a cold
passing
that stirred the fire. Sparks rose in a dust devil swirl.
He shivered as though touched by a phantom hand.
From somewhere across the mountain's flank, far off,
he heard, or thought he heard, the voice of a tracking
predator,

a long hound's call to the moon.
It's him, he thought.

The moon's horn split.
His eyes saw it, his mind recorded the impossible event
in the slow motion clarity of a psychedelic's dream
that has no reality and is reality itself. Everything
    was clear.
Abruptly, the upper prong of the convex moon broke in two
and from the division, fire and coals and sparks erupted
as though a rocket had burst. The moon's crescent writhed,
pulsed, and the sudden leap of flame, an instant in time
that seemed to him an hour, dwindled, died, and was replaced
by a spreading pall, a curtain that blanked the moon
and left it a shadow in the sky.
Was that the way it happened, the dinosaur's end?
The asteroid and the great encircling cloud of dust,
denying life?

In the morning, he found the tracks.
They were freshly made, embedded in the soft mantle of ash,
the sulphured blanket that covered the mountain grass,
the undergrowth and the flowers that should have been setting.
He skirted the windrows of fallen trees leveled by the
furnace wind,
came to a naked ridge and stood for a moment, looking down,
seeing the remains of a lifeless tarn.
There was no glint of water in its mud-filled bowl.
He'll be looking for a place to drink.
He'll have to escape this hell, go down to the meadows.
In a clearing beyond the ridge, once a
lovely place,
he saw a touch of green, an alien color in the gray waste,
a colony of lupine and red-thistled fireweed newly risen
from the ash. This earth will always live, despite the
eye's logic
of death, despite man's capability for annihilative chaos,
as long as the sun remains.

He walked to the east, returning.
He followed the hound's path, working down the course of
  a waterless canyon.
Twice he heard the dog's voice calling
and twice he listened for the answer that never came.
He's alone and he's searching.
In the late afternoon, the boy came to a grove of piñon pine,
a standing grove, sheltered by the spur of a mountain
  buttress,
spared from the volcanic wind and the devastating heat.
It was a good place, the trees widely spaced, and the ground
  between
softened by a layer of needles.
The dog's print showed clearly at the edge of a tiny spring.
The moon was veiled, but the veil tonight was gauze.

He was not prepared for the owl's rush.
Kneeling, tending the fire with his back to the night,
he heard nothing until the owl, diving, braked its assault

with outspread wings. He heard the air strike feathers,
was stunned by the blow of legs extended
and spurs that gashed his head.
Falling, he saw the attacker rise on silent wings,
vanishing into the darkness beyond the trees.
He was bleeding. He was not badly hurt.
The strangeness of it, the suddenness.
He rationalized that any living thing, in a land devoid of
quarry,
might attack an unaccustomed prey, even man
if its hunger were great enough.
He kept his eyes on the dark, guarding himself,
finished his supper and made his bed in a protected place.
The North Star was a reassuring friend.
As sleep came slowly, he let his mind wander into realms
of fantasy that have no answers.
Does the eye of an owl see beauty?
Does he know the majesty of stars, the distant silhouette
of a mountain ridge, darkest of all, that gives dimension
to the night?

Is beauty man's invention?

Westward, struck against the sky,
was the blasted cone of the once symmetrical mountain.
He lay in the grass, listening to the song of a cress-banked
stream
as it flowed through meadows, rattling the pebbles
that lined its bed, never in a hurry to join the infant river
in the valley below the last range of hills.
He'll have good hunting now; this land's not been touched.
He saw him once, a gray shadow in the sun,
and wondered where the hunt would end.
The soft, ever changing clouds were like the clouds of home,
telling endless stories,
bringing dreams and summer peace, and gladness.

That night the wind spoke in tongues.
He had found a long abandoned cabin that gave him shelter.

The storm had come swiftly, bringing rain
    and flooding,
and blasts of wind that bent the trees, breaking limbs,
He's holed up somewhere; he won't be moving in this.
The fire shadows played in the rafters, creating spectral
    shapes.
The warm rain-wind whistled through chinks in the walls,
stirring the fire. A drip of water from the weathered roof
made a steady tattoo on the hearth.
He imagined voices in the raging gusts that shook the cabin.
Once he heard a high, shrill cry for help.
Hell, it's nothing, just branches rubbing.
He slept poorly, waking often, hearing the storm.
In the quiet of a lull, he came fully awake,
eyes searching the darkened cabin.
He knew without seeing that someone, or something, was in
    the room.
The sense of a stranger's presence was strong, infesting
    the cabin
with an aura as pungent as sulphur gas.

He brought the fire to life. An old planked table caught
his eye.
It was moving, as though guided by an invisible hand.
As he watched, shrinking back, hand groping for a wooden poker,
the table buckled and fell as a leg collapsed.
He looked for the eyes that his sense imagined, seeing none.
He was alone, seeking logic that came slowly.
As the fire grew and the room lightened, the alien's presence,
waning,
was replaced with a chilling memory of something that was
and could not be.
When a great storm strikes and the wind talks
and your world becomes an island in a sea of chaos,
cut off, isolated, scourged by incantations of an unknown
origin
that make the night an evil force,
it is not difficult to believe that something exists
that transcends man's knowledge of science and religion.
He wished, then, that he had faith in God;
he would pray and the prayer would give him solace.

Fear is the genesis of religion.
The Maya knew that, creating gods to match their needs,
giving to themselves the power to govern.
Gods are the creation of man and could not exist
        without man's fear.

He smoked again, warming himself by the fire, conscious
of the storm's return, hearing the crash of a forest tree.
As he drifted into reverie, an illusion of sound possessed him.
He heard the grating rasp, as though talons were clutching,
ripping at the shingles that roofed the cabin.
A dreamworld fantasy, a conjuring of unreality.
In the morning, he would find that four cedar shingles,
old and warped and weathered thin,
had been torn from the leeward edge of the roof.

The dinosaur knew this place.
Its history is recorded in sandstone layers created by

ancient seas.
It was different then, a land of tropic swamps
before man's time, before the crustal buckling and building
of mountains.
He rested on the crest of a hill, seeing the river below him
and the great, open sweep of land beyond.
He knows that I'm coming; he'll have to swim across.
The track had been easy to follow, the soil softened by rain.
Drops of blood told that sometime, before storm's
end,
the dog had been wounded.
It doesn't look serious, a small cut probably.
Nothing to slow him down.
If he crosses the river, I've got him;
he'll be easy to spot in the open.

The mountain ridges, forested, gave way to grassland hills,
soft and sensuous, that flowed down to the river valley, to
meadows

rich with flowers of spring —
the time of rebirth and the murmur of bees in wild clover.
The river's course was masked in places by cottonwoods and aspen
crowding the water's edge. The far bank was different, treeless,
the beginning of the sagebrush plateau of the semi-desert.
He liked the place,
the abrupt dividing of ecologic zones, as though nature had meant,
in one sweeping panorama, to show the complexity of her art.
The green of trees and grass, the silver-gray of sage.

The river was close to flood,
turgid, roiled, dark with mountain silt, eddies boiling
in sudden upthrust wellings as though a fish of enormous size
were churning the water. Riverbank logs and broken limbs
swirled in crazy patterns.
The dog's track followed the river

along the bank between the water and the willows.
He's looking for a crossing.
At a place where the river curved, its force expended
against the far bank, a backwater eddy was a quiet pool.
The track ended there,
at the edge of the water, on a sandy shelf.
He's a brave old bastard
or he's running scared.
The boy studied the river, knowing that he could swim it
if he didn't force the current, just let it carry him,
in its time, at its choosing, to the opposite bank
downstream.

He made a simple raft, a makeshift thing of branches bound
together
with reeds and strips of willow sapling. He tied the bedroll
and his rifle to the flimsy platform, stripped and stuffed
the clothes in his canvas pack. The body was young,
clean, subtly muscled. Even the flesh of the buttocks was

brown.

He placed the raft in the water, laying the pack on top,
unsecured, and let his body slide into the river. The shock
of sudden cold engulfed him. *Hell, he's a damnsite luckier
than me; he's got a coat.*
Kicking gently, guiding the raft, holding the pack steady,
he moved away from the bank, swimming with the gentle
backwater current.
When the raft met the juncture of the river's main force,
the swifter current swung him in a circle.
He saw, looking back, on a high limb of an alder,
the figure of an owl. It was watching him, unblinking.
The raft, caught by the flood, was carried beyond the bend.
Ahead, the river was a long straight run of whitewater rapids.
Damn! It'll be a hell of a ride.
He was buffeted by the breaking water, choked, his leg bruised
by an unseen rock. Fighting the rapids, relying on the
strength
and the confidence of youth, he kept his grip on the raft
and his hand on the pack. He angled towards the bank,

trying to avoid the worst of the rapids. The river narrowed.
The force of raging water strengthened. Too late, he saw
    ahead
the massive shape of a river-smoothed boulder.
The raft brushed against the granite surface, raced down
a chute of plunging, skin-tight water into the vortex
below the rock. The raft, torn from his hand, overturned
and broke apart. Somehow, without conscious thought,
he kept his hold on the pack, jamming it against his body.
Beyond the cauldron, the river widened, slowed, the water
    calmed.
Using the pack as a float,
he forced himself to the sagebrush bank.

The warm sun dried his clothes.
He was pleased that his notebook, cased in a plastic bag,
had survived the crossing; the pencilled notations
were still fresh, not blurred by water. He bandaged the leg,
protecting the bruise, dressed and searched along the bank.

If he made it, he'll have to come out somewhere close.
The alluvial bank, high and steep, was a scarp of glacial
    debris,
quartzite pebbles, the detrital remains of a mountain worn
    down
by time and vanished.
He found the place. The stones were still wet where the dog
had shaken water from his coat before starting the climb
to the dry plateau above.
When he's thirsty, will he remember the river?
Is it memory or instinct?
After the sun had done its work, he repacked and set himself
to fashioning arrows and a simple bow. *The rifle's gone;*
I'll hunt like an Indian.
He rested awhile, content in the knowledge that his quarry,
after the river ordeal, would be moving slowly, warming himself
in the sun.

Venus was the brightest star.

The sagebrush night was soft and quiet, save the occasional
rustle
of a scurrying animal and the one-note voice of a bird
before sleep.
He relived the crossing, remembering the water's force,
the cold and the rapids, the cauldron and the calm. That
was good,
a good fight, just himself and nature.
I'd rather that, than be killed in a war.
He finished the last, banked the fire and prepared for the
dreams
that he hoped would come. Of Sheila and the stream-side cabin
and the peace of a land untouched by cities.
Almost dreaming, he heard the quavering howl of a coyote
answered by another, joined by the pack, then silence.
I wonder.
If he weren't being hunted, would he try to mate?
I guess he would.
Rogue dogs, he knew, sometimes lived in concert
with their wild brethren.

From a high point of land,
he looked across the sage-dappled plateau, morning clear,
to a far line of hills a day's march distant.
He looked for signs of water. In a shallow, dry ravine
that cut across the semi-desert country, running
towards the hills,
he saw a stand of willows that marked a spring, and beyond,
another.
He'll be making for that; he's thirsty.
An elk trail, arrow straight in places, led to the willows.
The dog would be searching, led by smell not reasoning,
doubling back from time to time, finding his direction again,
always moving, driven.
He saw him briefly, about a mile away, the tawny coat
a glint in the sage.
The dog could neither see the trail nor suspect.
The boy tightened his pack, scrambled down a rock slope,
gaining the path that led to the spring.
I'll beat him to it
if I go like hell.

Alternately he ran, then slowed to a walk, then ran again,
keeping his body low, using the shrubs to mask his presence.
When he neared the ravine, he circled left, leaving the trail,
working downwind, making for the far side of the willows.
The spring was a clear pool, its banks worn by the hoofs
of elk. Working fast, he devised a hiding place,
a concealment in the willows that gave him a view of the water
and a clear path for his arrow.
It'll be an easy shot, when he comes.
He saw the dog before he heard him, a shape materialized,
suddenly apparent against the backdrop of willows.
My God!
He's big as a pony.
The dog stood without moving, his quiet hound eyes searching
the pond and the willows for danger.
Cautiously, then, he stepped towards the water, lowering his
    head to drink.
The gold-gray coat was streaked with sweat. The rib cage
    showed
in the food craved body.

I'll let him drink, he deserves it.

When the dog's thirst was sated, he sat on the bank, on his
haunches,

giving the impression of a wise man deep in thought.

The boy readied his weapon, aligned the bow, drew the arrow
slowly,

avoiding movement.

An owl's screech! Wings beat against his face, smothering

the cry of suprise. The bow was ripped from
his hands

by clutching talons. The dog, rising,

was gone in a single leap.

A dog and an owl?

They'd never believe me.

He recorded the event in his notebook, shaking his head.

There's no point following now. I can't suprise him.

I'll give him a day's rest.

A strange thought came to him then, was rejected,

then accepted with reluctance.
He wrote: Could there be a time when animals, sensing
    man's power
for life's destruction, cooperate for their own protection?
Ridiculous.
At dusk, a sage hen come to water
was killed for the evening meal.

Beyond the hills, the desert.
The realm of enormous space, beckoning with the promise
of lost cities and green canyons that cannot exist,
leading the traveler through a fantasy of mesas, buttes,
and the silence of vastness.
The desert night is made for thoughts; the loneness and the
    stars.
Sheet lightning, as though conceived by a master pyrotechnist,
cast a monolithic spire in silhouette, a soaring
needle of wind-eroded sandstone capped with a basalt pediment,
with a curtain of fire its backdrop.

He thought of the trinity: the universe, the invention of
religion,
man's proclivity for war that is unique on earth.
What lies beyond the stars, the incredulity of endless space?
No mind can cope with that; there's a blindness in man's
ability
to comprehend. He is not perfect, and from imperfection
comes the awe
in which he holds the otherness of nature.
Awe dictates the need for gods.
The god of rain — the Maya called him Chac — may have been
the first,
the first conscious god of man's invention:
an idol or a stone for supplication, and sometimes sacrifice
to assure the amplitude of rain.
The conceptual ideality of god is unique to man.
Before his coming, there were no gods; the animals are
godless
and evolution progressed without the need for religion's
solace.

Man's reasoning mind, awed by mysteries and emotions
he cannot truly fathom, created gods and made them real.
There is no God.
There is a God.
Thunder sounded in the desert, the bass drum echoing
of nature's opera in the climax of performance.
War is the province of man, in a sense itself religion,
a transient suspension of uncertainties, a compression
of diverse concepts, fears, in a single purpose,
giving direction to existence.
Can man survive his own capacity for destruction?
He has no greater task — to somehow twist the atom's power
to nullify itself in terms of annihilation
and the final war.
Man has the genius. There's hope in that.

The dawn wind had stripped the soil.
The tracks ended at a place of kill, a bench of sandstone,
naked rock, swirled in layers, that was bare of prints.

The dog had eaten there. The bones and fur of small
nocturnal animals
were strewn at random. There was strangeness in it,
as though the feast, gathered at night across the desert floor,
has been assembled with conscious purpose
for the dog's support.
The day was hot, arid hot. The boy removed his pack,
stowed it in a cleft. He would search for tracks
at the base of the sedimentary hill, along the junipers
that divided the outcropped stone and the desert proper.
He would not return until the tracks had been found again
and the dog's intention known.
The sun was low when he came back to the sandstone bench.
What the hell!
His pack was ripped apart, mutilated, torn by an animal's
teeth.
His packets of raisins and jerky were opened, destroyed,
and the matches for his evening fire were gone entirely.
Stunned, he looked across the desert, knowing the inhumanity.
God damn you, bastard!

Somewhere across the desert
beyond the distant hills, the alkaline hills shining white
like the ramparts of an empire
soon to come ablaze with the sunset's magic,
he knew there would be a pueblo or a hogan with rising
    smoke.
There he could find supplies, and talk.
It was survival now, not chase.
He would travel at night, saving himself from the dessicating
heat of day. The desert was an adversary. He told himself
    that later,
after his return, he would recall the fight with pleasure.
Damn the dog; he's smarter than I thought.
There was no power on earth, no god that he could call upon.
It was he, himself, nothing more.

In the light of the false dawn,
as he made a place for sleep, shaded against the coming sun,
he imagined that he saw, briefly against the sky,

the figure of an owl in flight.
And heard, as though in dream,
a dog's voice, a questing howl
in the dark behind him.

He had come to the Old Place,
the stone masonry ruins in a watered valley, the ancient
    remnants
of a people, vanished, who had populated the desert's edge,
trading, growing crops
until the devastation of drought, as told in the rings of
    trees,
had forced the abandonment of their once proud centers.
He slept, not waking until the sun was high.
He searched the ruins for an archaeologist's cache, finding
    none.
The water in the valley's meagre stream was bitter,
but he drank and filled the canteen to its brim.
As he waited for the sun's decline, he thought:

The game's over, it's finished.
I'm almost glad that he won.
And he thought of the Old Ones, the ancients who had lived
here once.
They had gods, many, enough to crowd their kivas
when they chanted prayers in their own communal fashion.
The gods had not surmounted;
nature had.

The full desert moon,
shining again without its pall, made the desert
floor
almost as bright as day. He walked, guided by the stars,
and sometimes he ran. The memory was very much alive,
of the dog standing at dusk on a crumbled wall of the Old
Place
under the valley's cliff, watching.
There was no explanation for it, nothing rational. The dog,
it seemed,

had become the hunter, he the prey.
It's crazy.
His food was gone, arrows snapped, his bow made useless,
as though the dog had reversed the roles with reasoning
    thought.
The knife was his last defense,
if he weren't caught by surprise, sleeping.
Salvation would be an Indian's hogan.
He drove himself, moving east, hearing behind him,
or imagining, the panting of a hunting dog, and from time
    to time,
an owl's screech at the kill.

In the sun-crazed heat of day,
he lay protected by an overhang of rock, stones arranged
in a defensive wall. He would sleep, shepherding his strength,
knowing himself safe for a time at least.
The knife was fixed to his wrist with a leather thong.
They'll be wondering where I am.

They'll never find me here.

Dreams came to him, heat inspired dreams, almost psychedelic,
with vivid colors and changing images having no cohesive
meaning.
Once he dreamed of Sheila, seeing her face again,
knowing her love and his for her,
and he dreamed of food.

The night call of a predator coyote,
like the voice of an alien creature,
emphasized his loneness and the panic that he fought against.
He's out there somewhere, I know it.
The dog was a tangible presence now, a dark reality in the
night,
stalking,
somewhere close, unseen,
a picture in the mind of death and mutilation.
The boy stumbled often, his weakened body crying out for
sustenance.

He could not hide;
the dog's eyes were the owl's eyes that are made for night.
It can't be helped, I have to rest.
In a clump of thorned mesquite that would slow the dog's rush,
he scooped a trench in the sand and waited —
for the day's coming or the climax.
He found it hard to think coherently, blaming
the hunger and the sun fever that shook his body.
Dammit, he's a cunning sonofabitch.
He pictured the beast, the gold coat showing gray on top,
the eyes warm, like a woman's, or hard and passionless
when he set himself for the kill. *He'd have killed again*
if I hadn't stopped him.
Is he really there? Am I dreaming this?
He remembered his room at home, the parlor with lace-fringed
 curtains,
the damnfool minister who had almost tricked him into
 confirmation,
his own pleasure in seeing the mountains,
knowing them more permanent than man, but also doomed

by nature's law of change.
The coyote call was closer now,
the many-voiced call of a closing pack.
He told himself, the idea's nuts.
Have they joined against me, too?

The stream in the canyon bed,
a silver mosaic of shallow, meandering channels,
was lined with cottonwoods and there were patches of wild
onion and grass
in the small fields under the sheer-rising cliffs.
Had he walked a few more steps in the night, he would have
fallen.
The canyon wall dropped vertically below him, a thousand feet
of massive beauty, sandstone carved and polished, sensuous,
smooth, shaped by windborne sand.
Where the sun had not yet touched the cliffs, the shadows
were black.
Across the canyon, somewhere beyond the far rim,

smoke was rising in the morning sky.

He found a shepherd's trail,
a desperate path leading down into the canyon's depth
along angled, rock-choked fissures in the wall, sometimes
crossing
an open face of stone that would become impassible
in a rain, too slippery for a foothold.
Sometimes he lost the way, had to climb again,
his body protesting punishment.
The green promise of a watered field gave him back,
superficially,
the strength that he had lost to the desert.
When the trail came to the canyon floor, at the mouth of a
side ravine,
he rested, drinking from the brackish stream, clearing his
head
with the cooling water.
The cottonwoods gave him shade.

The wild onions were bittersweet. He dared not eat too much,
just a little at a time.

The cliffs were fortress walls,
deep cut by cloudburst floods through eons of time.
The summer stream was shallow, a thin, liquid film on the
sand.
He began the crossing. Somewhere in the far shadows,
another trail would climb the opposing wall,
taking him close to the smoke that he had seen from the rim.
He was not thinking rationally, the fever a pulsing beat.
He felt himself sinking,
felt the liquid sand closing around his ankles,
sucking, drawing his body down.
The sudden shock of enormous danger cleared his mind.
Reacting, he threw himself face down, spreading
his weight,
trying to keep himself above the treacherous surface of
the canyon floor.

His hands clawed the sand, inching his body out of the
quicksand trap.
The boots, stripped from his feet, were lost under the sand
that had no bottom.
He lay in the sparse grass of the stream bank, exhausted.
The shadow of an owl crossed his face.

Stark, unreasoning panic.
The dog was crouched by the side of a fallen rock.
The boy ran, not conscious of the stones that cut his feet,
knowing only that survival meant a place of refuge.
He ran along the base of the cliff, along a narrow strip
between the great wall and the stream, on a path made by
sheep.
When he could run no more, he walked,
forcing his mind to think.
His feet were bleeding now and he felt the pain.
If he found a place to cross, he wouldn't have the strength
to climb the impossible trail

that would lead vertically out of the canyon.
Shit! He's got me trapped.
The strip of land widened to a field. He came to an orchard,
the peach trees dead, abandoned.
The sandstone cliff, curving outward, softly graceful,
dwarfed the trees and made them tiny.
The sky was immeasurably far away.
On a ledge above the canyon floor, sheltered by the overhang,
ancient masonry buildings, meticulously crafted, lifeless,
were little changed since their time of building,
never disturbed by the Indians who fear their spirits
and respect the ancestral dead.
A rock slope, cut in places with occasional hand and toeholds,
served as a primitive staircase.
The boy climbed,
sensing for the first time that he had found a place of
    safety.
He can't follow; it's too damn steep.
The dog waited, resting in a cottonwood's shade,
eyes following the boy's climb.

He could survive.

The canteen was full, he had saved a dozen wild onions.

I'll figure a way out, in the morning.

The building he had chosen was a barren place,

a single room with an opening facing the canyon.

It was dark, a relief from the brilliant sun. The back wall

was the cliff itself. The sides and front were made of thin,
    rectangular

blocks of sandstone fitted precisely together.

People had lived there once, a thousand years past.

The rock wall was stained by smoke.

He tore his shirt into strips, bandaging his feet.

From the doorway, he could see the complex of buildings,

the tall centerpiece tower, three stories with a tiny window
    at each floor,

the circular kivas open to the sky,

all of the structures built on the ledge, above the

flash flood line of torrents that periodically inflict
    the canyon

with their stone-carving power.

He robbed an adjacent building of loose stones,
making a barricade.
It was time to rest, and plan.

The moon rose early,
flooding the canyon with golden light, converting the great
    stone cliffs
into a sculpture of enormous beauty.
The peach trees in the orchard below were black skeletons
standing in translucent pools.
When the fever shook his body, he drank sparingly.
Thoughts of home crowded his mind, the white church
with its steeple pointing to a heaven imagined, not real.
The bridge across the river where they had stood together,
dreaming of their lives ahead.
The sheep in the pastures and the wild geese flying.
He thought of the people who had once made the canyon their
    home.
Their gods were the gods of the seasons,

of childbirth and death,
the primitive gods of a primitive religion.
Once he heard voices and was afraid,
imagining a circle of tribal men gathered together
in the central kiva, chanting, performing rites,
beseeching the gods for the rain that would not come.
One foot had festered. Its pain was the link to reality.
That and the hunger.
In the Maya world, the gods became demanding,
demanding impossibilities for the priestly rulers who spoke
  for them.
The people rose,
destroying their rulers and their templed civilization.
Sleeping, the boy dreamed of the coyote pack, heard the long
  quavering howl
and the deeper voice of the dog.

A premonition of danger awoke him.
The night was silent. There was no wind, no movement, no

sound.
He sensed that silent eyes were gathered in the darkness,
told himself that it was only his mind imagining,
was drawn to the barricaded doorway,
to the ledge, to a place where the canyon floor was exposed
in the moon's brilliance.
He saw them then, at the base of the slope below the
dwellings,
the pack ringed in a half circle, sentinals on guard,
waiting.
The figure of the dog was large among them.

The rock walls of the canyon
were already heating in the morning sun when he returned to
the ledge.
The pack was gone, and the dog. *He's sleeping.*
Now's the chance.
The shepherd's trail followed the stream course, coming
to a place where the canyon narrowed. It crossed there,

a floor of sandstone providing a firm, safe base.
He studied the trail, seeing where it disappeared in a shadowed
side canyon, hoping that it led to the rim, up close to the sky,
to the hogan that he pictured in his mind.
He secured the canteen to his belt and started down,
taking each step one at a time, sparing his feet, not trusting
the strength in his wasted body,
using the ancient handholds where the rock was steep.
He paused before reaching the bottom. The slope was a gentle gradient now,
only a hundred yards down to the canyon floor and the shepherd's trail.
He looked for the dog in the cottonwoods, seeing nothing.
Jesus Christ!
The rock slope below him, smooth and polished with the desert's patina,
was alive with snakes, rattles glistening,

a deadly army in the sun.
He dared not challenge; without boots, the poisoned fangs
would lacerate his feet, bringing death.
There's got to be a way.
Tonight maybe, if the dog's not back, the goddamn rattlers
won't be out.
He forced himself to climb, step by agonizing step,
his mind a jumbled chaos.
The chance of survival was slim; water nearly gone,
no food and the fever growing.
Had the dog led him here, and the owl perhaps, for this?
Had he always been the hunted?
Not the hunter?

The dark room was refuge,
an ephemeral respite from the death that existed
in the canyon,
in the bright sun under the living walls of rock.
He felt the hunger and the thirst. There was no escape,

just the waiting and the hopelessness.

And the fear.

The room itself a tomb.

A spasm of fever wracked his body and he drank the last few
drops of water.

He was trapped; there was no living power to help him.

He thought of miracles, the last resort,

the impossibility of salvation, supernaturally derived,

that has comforted man through all of his civilizations,

a light in the sunless hours.

The words came to him slowly, long forgotten, long denied.

He began, kneeling in the darkness of the rock-walled room:

Our Father who art in heaven —

An owl rose in the day sky, circling,
gaining the canyon rim, flying west toward the unseen
    mountains,
the pines and the lakes and the stream that he loved,
and Sheila so far away.
A Navajo shepherd, coming down from the plateau above,
brought his flock to water.

    No one ever knew.
The story was never told, never revealed, not even to her.
He had followed the dog to the desert, had lost his way.
There was nothing more,
no mention of the shepherd's coming.
Sometimes, when the church bells rang and summer clouds were
    piled in the sky,
he remembered the dog and the owl
and thought of powers beyond the scope of mortal logic.
There is no God.
Man cannot live without Him.

THE END

FIRST EDITION 1984

One Thousand copies. Body type, 12-point Sabon; display face, New Caslon Black.
Typography by Monterey Graphics, Monterey, California.
Printed by Herald Printers, Monterey.
Design by Colden Whitman